About the Author

S. Elizabeth Cook is an award-winning author and poet of four published poetry collections, the most recent being *Yellow Light*. A true romantic, S. Elizabeth has spent nearly a decade writing about and capturing the raw existence of humans, nature and love. She believes there is beauty in heartache and a deflating pain in love, and that one must fall to let it hurt.

S. Elizabeth Cook maintains a daily haiku project on Instagram: @s.elizabethcook.

Before You Go

S. Elizabeth Cook

Before You Go

Olympia Publishers
London

www.olympiapublishers.com
OLYMPIA PAPERBACK EDITION

A CIP catalogue record for this title is
available from the British Library.

ISBN: 978-1-80074-287-1

First published in 2021

Olympia Publishers
Tallis House
2 Tallis Street
London
EC4Y 0AB

Printed in Great Britain

Dedication

To love, life and beyond.

Acknowledgements

For Mom and Dad, there will never be enough words to express my deepest gratitude and love for you. Thank you for loving and trusting me without boundaries and giving me a runway to chase my passions and dreams.

For all I have loved, for all I have lost, for all I have seen, and for all I have held

For Leigh, my stunning and forever partner. Words were just words before you. Thank you for bringing meaning and weight to my writing.

There's only one truth.
You'll leave, but before you go,
find her, leave her wild.

How quickly I learned
envy when the page held
you longer than me.

I will practice the
way I fall into her till
it's second nature.

Soaking inside you,
prepared to bear storms waiting.
I ran for cover.

Run not from the night.
Remember the time before,
each morning will come.

No longer can I
sit and watch the wind touch you
in ways I forgot.

I may get tired.
This anxious skin tends to run.
Calm me with your time.

Hold on to the dream
stirred in your tea each morning.
Taste all that you'll chase.

Extend my limbs for
the warmth settling in you.
Baby, please come home.

Wake me up for this.
Take your limbs and wrap me up.
Baby, I came home.

Tired hands can't rest
without the deafening sound
playing in your breath.

I will now stay warm
without your emptying touch.
I will wait no more.

Of all the treasures,
the monuments my eyes find.
You're always enough.

Need not just one day.
{ There's too much of you and not
enough ways to hold.

What a way to go.
Recklessly crawling towards home,
wait for me to go.

How the magic plays
with a Sunday kind of love.
Half-naked and tough.

You said I lost it.
All this promise wasted from
being exhausted.

Skin so delicate
in the morning before I
stretch it out to you.

Even in shadows
you spill every ounce of light.
It's time I came home.

Fancy words won't do.
I cannot hide behind them.
I simply love you.

It aches to wake when
each morning you are not there.
Baby, I'm home sick.

Forget the science,
or divine intervention.
I believe in love.

There's plenty of time
for our lips to move closer.
I will take it all.

The air has now thinned.
All my chest needed was to
feel your breath near me.

I'll no longer wait,
or chase the dreams in my sleep.
I'll reach them awake.

I saw the magic
across the eyes you tried to
keep away from me.

How quick must I be
to catch you before time steals
this away from me?

How can you not see
you're your own blanket of stars?
Your light is enough.

This time, I will leave.
Loving you is too heavy,
and I cannot breathe.

You still do not know
the rarity pouring from
you being so close.

Can we slow it down?
Go around the sun once more
before morning comes?

How much will you hold,
before your shoulders grow weak
carrying me home?

When it's time to go.
Wherever I roam, I will
hold these napkins close.

I'm finally here.
My skin does not shake with fears
because she found me.

I wake and rustle.
Being too far leaves cold sheets.
I need you closer.

It's overwhelming,
you don't see how you hold me.
You should have warned me.

It's neither the heights
or the fall that frightens me,
if you're catching me. ♡

How many mornings
must I wait to wake with you
before I have you?

I feel the cold breeze,
emptiness born in the sheets.
I'll keep your side warm.

Morning will not wait.
The magic is waking up
knowing it's enough.

We have reached the end.
Where the road empties my skin.
I've no use for this.

The war in your mind
needed lies to sleep at night.
Leave me out of it.

The road deserves us.
The adventure begs our feet.
Come away with me.

What a disservice,
to deny my cowardice ways.
I, too, beg to change.

How many more lies
will stuff my tongue and pretend
that was the last time?

You were so precise
in how you moved through your game.
I am done playing.

Do not wake just yet.
Before we must rise from bed,
let us wreck the sheets.

The smoke attested
to how you always linger,
how you always rise.

Tangled legs and hair.
You wrapped inside my fingers.
How else could I sleep?

Of all the noise here,
your voice is the only one.
My ears feel you move.

My lips to your neck.
With your skin under my nails.
Each morning I wake.

If I dare to melt,
plunge myself within your skin,
will you soak in me?

A quiet stirring
following our wakeful night.
Sleep is for the lonely.

Your eyes like shovels,
hands eager to get dirty,
reached deep to find me.

Clothes hitting the floor,
relieving sighs flee your mouth.
The most thrilling sounds.

Through all of the times,
from the start to the ending,
I need you with me.

I need you to know,
no matter how far I stray,
I will still miss home.

There's not enough skin.
I want all of mine on yours.
How do I get more?

Whether it's the road,
or the bed your toes stay on.
I will follow you.

She would be the wind.
All she needed was a storm.
Oh, how she was wild.

Stuck in my daydream
with closed eyes, hoping each night
I'm not wasting it.

No matter the speed.
The stillness or the bustle.
I'll stay beside you.

How much time is left
before it's out and my mouth
can't find the next breath?

I'm made of much more
than you could ever believe.
No mountain's too steep.

Silence is louder
when the space between us grows.
Can you hear it scream?

If the night sweats come,
and my nature is to run,
will you hold me tight?

The frost is coming.
Come take shelter in my arms,
and we'll thaw the sheets.

It was just as quick
as a leaf tumbling down.
My falling for you.

I can't close my eyes
without you standing near me.
How could I escape?

Now, more than ever,
do I wish to be the sun.
Pulling you from sleep.

There is a roughness
living on top of your lips.
Each kiss before me.

It is this right here,
the spark you put in my bones,
that makes me miss home.

This is familiar,
waking up to the cold space.
It is all the same.

Now, there's just coffee
waking and staining my lips,
instead of your kiss.

When the wine runs out,
will there be anything left
to soak up your touch?

Go wander it all.
Climb too high and swim too far.
Just come home to me.

Where can I find them?
I don't have enough words to
fully sum you up.

Your lips pull away
with my breath following you.
Never give it back.

I'll unwrap no more.
Unless it's you underneath.
Baby, let's go home.

A surge in my skin
leaves me paralyzed in bed
when wrapped in your limbs.

Even in this blur,
you will stay the focal point.
My eyes won't dare shift.

I have the patience.
Waiting does not deter me
from staying with her.

Let's steal afternoons.
Quick fixes of our kisses.
Before we must work.

As springtime creeps up,
the smell of the warm wind feels
like you're here again.

It's not just today.
But every moment year-round
this love deserves praise.

Your subtle movement
in the bed to let me know
this isn't a dream.

The crick in my neck,
and the breath escaping me,
from watching you leave.

Your lips and your neck,
a canvas for me to paint.
To stain with a kiss.

I can feel your kiss,
long after you pull away,
sticking to my skin.

Never could I rid,
and never will I wish to,
this hunger for you.

I'll know the whole world.
And find the quiet of home.
They are both in you.

Like puddles on streets,
my lips will settle on you,
where kisses play.

I've these roving eyes.
Give me miles and miles of you.
I'll see all I need.

It has to be you.
My legs are too dubious.
You must walk away.

Our lips will not shift,
as if secrets might spill out.
I'll kiss you longer.

A stark wildfire,
the faint sound of spring showers.
You are both, fiercely.

There is no steeple
my knees will surrender to.
It is only you.

It is in your hands,
that I am both unraveled
and held together.

There is no more room.
My thoughts cannot move an inch
without finding you.

This skin I'm wearing,
it's unrecognizable.
It does not fit me.

Take the time to grow.
You need roots before branches,
seeds before the stem.

I try to fit you,
capture you in three small lines.
I will keep trying.

There is no distance.
No wide road or deep ocean.
To keep me from you.

Let us take it slow.
Before we must rise from bed,
let's make morning wait.

Spread across my face,
she was the warm yellow light
even suns envied.

If you're the blank page,
permit my hands to be ink.
I will cover you.

I can't remember
when my hands have felt like mine.
It has been so long.

Hands fold out to her.
Like leaves turning in the fall.
Eager to uncurl.

A heart is a heart.
Each one born beating freely.
Love is love is love.

Holding me hostage.
The villain in the mirror.
Weaponizing me.

Guns tucked behind tongues.
We use curses like bullets.
A war in our home.

No battle unmet.
She fought with a truth and a force.
With us, and for us.

The storms in my head,
and the ones pillaging skies.
Where to seek shelter?

A day full with life.
To a night soft and quiet.
Each second with you.

Like collected dust.
Fingerprints cover my skin.
All the marks you left.

If I'm ever lost,
and need to find my way home.
I will look for you.

I knew just two truths.
Morning came, as mornings will.
Sheets still smelled of her.

My rough, reckless heart.
To your calm and steady soul,
You keep us balanced.

Soft as warm butter,
like smoothly woven velvet.
Her hands moved on me.

With pride, I'll wear them.
Battle scars, bruised and bloody.
When fighting for us.

A slow waking sun.
Your legs, and breath, lost on mine.
It must be Sunday.

Do you see it all?
All this open skin waiting?
It's yours to cover.

All together now.
Our hands must rebuild this home.
She is trusting us.

Like they never left.
Like they can't let go of you.
The way my hands move.

They tried with envy
to match storms we made in bed.
Waves crashing to shore.

I want less of it.
What is the point of this space,
if you don't fill it?

You covering me,
like dirt on skin during spring.
It just has to be.

A painted canvas.
Your skin spread out on the sheets.
What a masterpiece.

Did not know their strength
until they had something to lose.
My hands holding you.

We are like the birds.
Waking from the bitter cold.
Waiting to return.

Through times of trial,
it is your name I will cry.
When faith must be called.

They all take your shape.
Form in the sound of your name.
All the words I speak.

Bodies passing by,
with eyes and hands reaching out.
I only catch yours.

What makes it a home?
Holding brick by brick in place?
You, it's always you.

I looked up at her,
and I felt them roll down her.
Eyes like a landslide.

I tossed and I turned.
How could anyone get sleep
with you to unwrap?

Scatter across me.
Like creatures in your fingers
roaming in the night.

The lines on my face,
stories traced from love and joy.
From life spent with you.

Stuck, frozen in bed.
She held me, I held my breath.
Will one of us break?

One piece at a time.
From limb to limb, bone to bone.
Take me down easy.

What is this feeling?
A coldness I've never known.
My lips absent yours.

Till feet are blistered.
With miles and miles left to go.
I will run to you.

It will be my hands,
the morning will be too late,
waking you from sleep.

Time lost on her tongue.
Hours take shape of seconds.
How do I find more?

My lips now chapped
from my mouth not finding yours.
The sting of regret.

Is that how this ends?
Just one night tossed to the wind?
Is that all I was?

The pieces of you
I will travel; get to know.
I will take my time.

Only fools rush in
when your arms open that wide.
I'm not different.

There is only yours.
No other body, or mouth,
that my lips will touch.

Is it luck or greed?
To have the world in my hands,
to have you to hold?

My lips, if they stray,
maybe she will taste like you.
Like you, fill my mouth.

If this is fleeting,
let me get a final glance.
Just one more second.

We are far away.
Still, I can feel the earth shake
from each move she makes.

My eyes and my hands
cannot find a place to stick.
Cannot find your skin.

The way it lingered —
it staying longer than you —
your taste on my lips.

How much time must pass?
Before lips, skin, hands forget
how yours felt on them?

Like an aged red wine,
a taste I can't wash away.
You're stuck on my tongue.

> Your voice, like gospel.
> Those bones stronger than temples.
> How do I show praise?

Did they ever feel,
my hands, before touching you?
Were they ever full?

Morning is greedy
when it rips you from our bed.
Takes you from my arms.

One more ticking clock.
One more evening turned morning.
Again, without you.

{ Fingers weaved as one
play deafening melodies
heavens could not match.

And what would you say,
if the skin covering me
asked yours to come play?

How I will live life,
and the ways I will spend time.
On you and with you.

My words lose their sound.
Tripping over my own tongue,
when she is around.

Like the first snowfall,
sticking and freezing to streets,
your lips land on mine.

My fingers are weak,
holding onto you too tight.
It's time I release.

Your touch, sweet and smooth,
poured over me like honey.
Your skin stuck on mine.

Even sleepless eyes,
covered with tired eyelids,
will stay stuck on you.

Lend me all your faults.
My shoulders are strong enough,
I'll carry their weight.

Of all the lessons,
the things I have discovered,
I learned love with you.

I forget its sound —
my voice without you in it.
I'll learn it again.

Stay like a promise,
one that's louder than gospel.
Or, leave quietly.

Such insanity.
My hands reaching back for you,
like sea to the shore.

What to do with it?
This air, when you're not in it.
It's a waste of breath.

What is left to fear?
I can look pain in the face.
Nothing hurts like her.

My hands remain sore,
they are beaten and weary,
trying to reach yours.

There is no space left.
Not a single inch is free.
You fill all of me.

I'll lend you my eyes.
You can see yourself through them.
See all that I see.

After this life ends,
will you meet me in the next,
and all after that?

Of all I have seen,
of all places I've landed,
home was in her hands.

If not spent on yours,
what's the use of this body?
Where does it go now?

Which way do I go?
How do I get back to you?
What will pave the way?

I should've heard it.
The shaking inside her voice.
A loud warning sign.

It's just a body.
Used to replace your absence.
Keeping your side warm.

Where did the words go?
Did they follow your footsteps?
Are there any left?

Will morning know
where to paint its yellow light
now that you are gone?

Both fingers and hands
look better wrapped around you.
Please stay and fill them.

My hands are itching,
and my lips are quivering,
to take hold of you.

In the morning sun,
in the seconds before sleep,
will you stay for both?

This, I can't capture.
    I can't capitalize.
You leaving my grasp.

I will stretch my skin,
reach with extended fingers,
close the gap in bed.

Trails of your lip stains.
Remnants of your fingertips.
I'll wear nothing else.

Nothing compares to
the way you look beneath me.
My favorite view.

Go, if you must leave.
Follow where your toes lead you.
Still, come home to me.

Must I wake like this?
With empty arms and covers
when you once filled them?

The rain taunting me,
washing my touch off your skin.
When will this storm clear?

I'll always wonder.
What do these eyes have to see
if not met with yours?

There's no other sound
my ears will perk in praise for.
It's only your voice.

When it is my time,
I'll fall, wildly, into her.
Call it suicide.

Often I forget,
after bodies fill my hands,
I've skin of my own.

All the words I have,
and not one is good enough.
None worthy of you.

Your tongue explores me.
Unraveling limbs like thread.
Breaking me open.

There are words at rest,
kept hidden behind my teeth.
They're ready to play.

From fingers to toes.
All the spaces between them.
My body feels you.

My tongue is swollen,
and my fingers weighted down.
Stuffed with words for her.

Before it touched yours,
where was this body going?
What was it made for?

Can I find the words?
The ones you will fit in?
Should I even try?

What is of this bed,
if you don't fill the covers?
How would one get sleep?

Placed by my fingers,
her skin is lined with the words
my mouth could not speak.

Unavoidably,
my body fell into you.
Like snow melts to rain.

Is there enough ink?
Pages to hold onto you?
I will keep looking.

The space between us,
how quickly can I close it?
It teases my skin.

Hands must stay busy
to cover the emptiness
of not holding you.

Watch how the snow falls.
Do you see how effortless?
Like I fell for you.

No spot I will miss.
There's no corner of your skin
that I won't explore.

Don't leave me alone.
Leave behind traces of you
before you must go.

Hands sore and calloused,
bearing the weight of your skin.
I can hold no more.

With skin I'm wearing,
and the bones holding me up.
I'll build you a home.

Everyone should hold
a little bit of hope, and
a woman like you.

Does this world know?
Will it be ready to hold
this love inside me?

Each time you leave,
you take all the words with you.
You take part of me.

Can't keep my footing.
Stumble over and over
trying to reach you.

How quickly it came,
almost as quick as you left.
This cold in the air.

Too quickly I run.
Even quicker will I fall.
When will I settle?

I can feel the itch,
the stirring within my toes.
Where will they go next?

I'm nothing but words.
Still, I am left needing more
writing about her.

You sound like a prayer.
Hearing you, I hear heaven.
A hallelujah.

What an adventure,
charting through each freckle.
I'll leave none untouched.

Watch as my skin dries.
Get pulled back in and thrown out,
with those ocean eyes.

The hairs on my neck
stand tall in an ovation.
Begging an encore.

You can have my youth.
Give me time, give me wrinkles.
Give me life with you.

Your eyes like marbles,
so hesitant to touch me.
Roll across my skin.

Won't fit here or there.
My bones do not bend that way.
They don't fit your mold.

I knew there was more.
More beyond stale fairytales.
I knew she would come.